The Hidden Life of the
FOREST

Photographs by DWIGHT KUHN
Text by DAVID M. SCHWARTZ

CROWN PUBLISHERS, INC.
NEW YORK

To my wife and best friend, Kathy.
D.K.

For my friends Glenn and Inge, fellow explorers
of forests and other hidden worlds.
D.M.S.

Text copyright © 1988 by David Schwartz
Photographs copyright © 1988 by Dwight Kuhn
Black bear photograph © by Lynn Rodgers (Ely, Minnesota)

Concept development and photo/editorial coordination
by the Soderstrom Publishing Group Inc.

Published by Crown Publishers, Inc., 225 Park Avenue South, New York, New
York 10003 and represented in Canada by the Canadian MANDA Group
Limited

CROWN is a trademark of Crown Publishers, Inc.

Manufactured in Japan

Book design by Kathleen Westray and Ed Sturmer

Library of Congress Cataloging-in-Publication Data

Kuhn, Dwight. The hidden life of the forest/photographs by Dwight Kuhn;
text by David M. Schwartz.

Summary: Photographs and text introduce the animals, insects, and plants
in a forest.

1. Forest fauna—Juvenile literature. 2. Forest plants—Juvenile literature.
3. Forest ecology—Juvenile literature. [1. Forest animals. 2. Forest plants.
3. Forest ecology. 4. Ecology.] I. Schwartz, David M. II. Title.
QH541.5.F6K83 1988   574.5′2642   88-11865
ISBN 0-517-57058-0

10 9 8 7 6 5 4 3 2 1

First Edition

Black bear mother and cub

Cold, quiet, and draped with snow, the forest in winter appears still and lifeless. But is it? Some animals tunnel under the snow, searching for food all winter long. Animals like the black bear hibernate, often in caves and under stumps.

Ferns unfolding

Maple seedling

Red maple flower

With warmer weather, a surge of life comes to the forest. Plants whose green parts died in the fall send up new shoots. Each uncurling fern resembles the head of a violin and is called a fiddlehead.

Trees stand through the winter, but in spring their seeds come to life, sprouting roots and rising from the soil. Meanwhile, the maple's crimson flowers will develop into next year's crop of seeds. Once the blooms have wilted, the trees bud with new leaves.

Red maple tree

Robin with ten-day-old young

For birds, spring is the nesting season. Some nest in the treetops, some lower in branches, some just a foot or two above the forest floor, some right on the ground. The robin may nest almost anywhere.

The Nashville warbler builds its nests on the forest floor. With their mouths gaping wide, baby birds let their mothers know how hungry they are. Each nestling eats about half its own weight in food every day. Imagine how much you would have to eat if you needed that much food.

Nashville warbler

Wasp

The ichneumon *(ick-NEW-man)* wasp penetrates a tree's thick bark to lay her eggs in worm tunnels deep within the wood.

Male mosquitoes eat only nectar and other plant juices. The female mosquito needs blood to nourish her eggs. To get it, she pricks a victim's skin and sends down a long feeding tube. Inside the tube is a liquid that keeps the blood from clotting. It is this liquid that we find so itchy when we receive a mosquito bite.

Mosquito

Young bobcat

Born in spring, young bobcats stay near their mothers until late fall. In their first year, bobcats learn the essential skills of life—climbing trees and hunting for birds, mice, rabbits, and other small mammals. Bobcats also learn to be silent and secretive, and for that reason it is a rare treat to see one.

Barred owl

Cavities in trees make homes for many kinds of animals. Here, a young barred owl peers out of its nest.

Raccoons take shelter in many kinds of places, including people's basements and attics, but their favorite hideaway is a deep treehole in the woods.

Raccoon

A fawn browses on the forest's low-lying plants. Its spots will disappear before it is grown up, but in the meantime they help the animal blend in with the sun-speckled forest floor. While the fawn stands still, its tail hangs down, but at the first sign of danger, it goes up like a flag, warning other deer to beware.

Fawn

Anole lizards

Box turtle

At the edge of southern woodlands, lizards called anoles bask in the sun. Like chameleons, they are brown when relaxed, green when excited. Sticky toe pads help them keep their footing.

The box turtle may live for a hundred years. It eats earthworms, wild fruit, and other foods, and gains protection by drawing into the natural armor of its shell.

Many people think snakes are slimy. In fact, their skin is hard and glossy. As you grow, your skin grows with you. But snakes have a problem: they get bigger and bigger but the outer layers of their skin stay the same size. So, a snake must shed its skin several times a year. Beneath the skin, snakes are very muscular. Pound for pound, they have more muscle than almost any other animal.

Green snake shedding skin

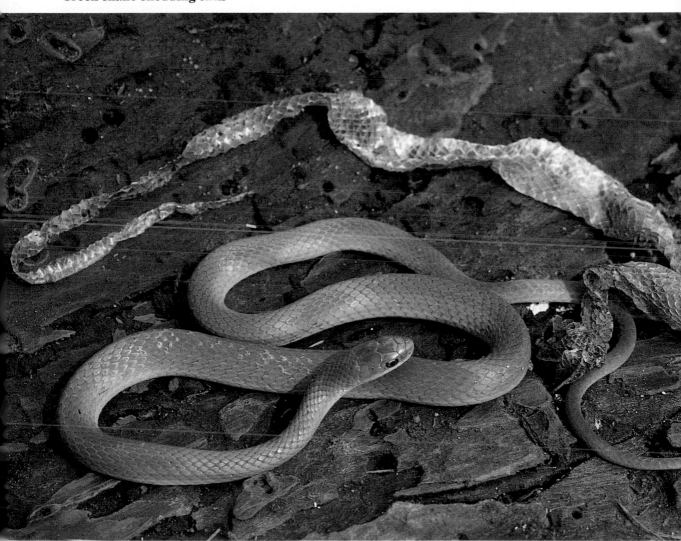

Gray treefrog

    Frightened by a predator, a gray treefrog makes a spectacular leap through the air. To land, it grabs hold of a branch with tiny suction cups on the tips of its toes. An airborne frog can't see because special muscles have pulled its eyes into their sockets to protect them from twigs and thorns. But when sitting still, a frog is very good at spotting flying insects. When a tasty-looking meal flies by, the frog flicks out its tongue, faster than the human eye can see.

Moth

Caterpillar emerging from egg

The life cycle of the beautiful cecropia moth is typical of most moths and butterflies. Females deposit eggs on a leaf.

Out of the egg crawls a larva—a small black caterpillar that devours practically every green thing in sight…

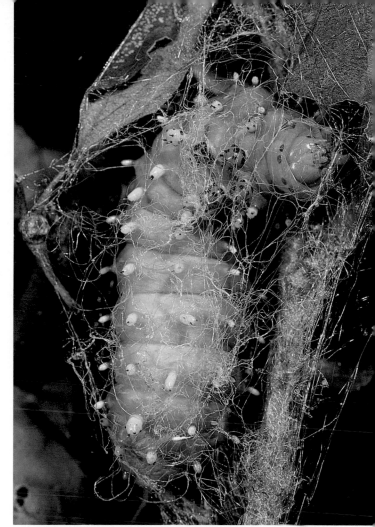

Caterpillar making cocoon

Cocoon

and soon turns green itself.

After several months of feeding, the caterpillar spins a silk cocoon around itself. Inside the cocoon, great changes are taking place. Next spring, a winged adult will emerge.

Lady's slippers

By early summer, lady's slippers have bloomed, ready to be admired by anyone lucky enough to find them. Beautiful as they are, lady's slippers are rare and should never be picked or dug up. If disturbed, they will quickly wilt. The only place they can survive is in their natural woodland habitat.

One of the strangest—and most common—forms of plant life is the lichen. Each lichen is actually two plants in one, a combination of a green alga and a fungus growing so closely together they cannot be separated. The alga, like all other green plants, makes food from sunlight, air, and water. The fungus, on the other hand, provides moisture and a protective environment. The arrangement works so well for both plants that lichens are found almost everywhere on earth—in desert sands, on arctic rocks, in tropical rainforests—even on the backs of giant tortoises!

Lichen

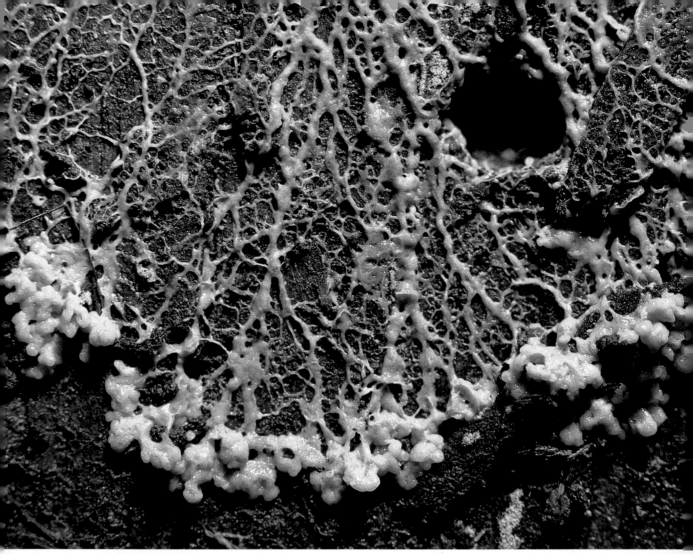

Slime mold

Strange as the lichen may be, the slime mold is even odder. It is so odd, in fact, that scientists can't decide whether it's a plant or an animal! The slime mold begins life as a single cell, swimming on dead leaves or on decaying logs in the shadiest parts of the forest. Eventually millions of these cells come together and form a slimy mass that creeps along, seeking rotten bits of wood, decaying leaves, and small mushrooms to eat. The slime mold eats by surrounding food and drawing it into its body.

Like slime molds, mushrooms thrive on dead plant matter. Some mushrooms grow on the forest floor, some grow on fallen logs, and some live on dead or dying trees.

Mushrooms

All living things contain energy. When they die, that energy is returned to nature and recycled into other living things. This important process of decay is called decomposition.

Fallen log on forest floor

Same log after seven years

Here, a fallen log is carpeted with soft green moss. The moss itself does not decay the log, but it creates an environment for slime molds, bacteria, fungi, and certain animals. You can see how this log has "shrunk" down into the ground. The many plants and animals living on it have reduced its size and returned much of its energy to the forest.

Sow bug

Turn over a fallen log and you'll likely find sow bugs, also known as woodlice. Not really insects at all, these animals are actually related to crabs and lobsters.

Ants also help attack decaying logs. They chew tunnels in the rotting wood, lay their eggs, and raise their brood.

The centipede, another rotten-log dweller, isn't at all interested in eating decaying wood, but it preys on sow bugs, ants, earthworms, and other creatures the log harbors. If you see a centipede, don't touch! Many kinds inflict a bite as painful as a wasp sting.

Ant

Centipede

Wolf spider with young

Another menace to insects is the brown wolf spider. They do not spin webs, but pounce upon their prey. Baby wolf spiders ride on their mother's back.

A slug is like a snail without a shell. Always in danger of drying out, they often inhabit moist, protected areas inside fallen logs.

Slug laying eggs

A red fox searches for its next meal at the forest's edge. These mammals are equally willing to crouch behind a log to ambush a mouse as they are to stand up on their hind legs to strip a wild bush of juicy berries. Because they are so adaptable, foxes have survived in forests around the world, but they have been wiped out in many areas. Although they have a reputation for raiding chicken coops, foxes eat thousands of mice and rats. They are valuable to people and to the forest.

Fox

In the north, you can tell the season by the weasel. In summer it's brown with a white belly, but in winter its fur turns white everywhere except for the tip of its tail. Weasels look cute, but they fiercely attack rabbits, rats, large birds, and other animals several times their size.

Like many small mammals, the short-tail shrew is both predator and prey. This pointy-nosed bundle of energy races back and forth, sometimes on the ground, sometimes in tunnels, feeding furiously on worms, insects, and mice. But the shrew must be careful or it will end up as a meal for a weasel, fox, or owl.

Weasel

Short-tail shrew

Saw-whet owl

The saw-whet owl has just what it takes to be a nighttime hunter. Its huge eyes are so good at collecting light that they can make out shapes in one-hundredth the light that humans require.

If an owl wants to see behind its back, it can turn its head all the way around. Its ears are so sensitive that it can hear a deer mouse step on a leaf seventy-five feet away. Even if blindfolded, the owl could fly right to the mouse.

But such extraordinary skill is not enough. Unless the mouse is surprised, it will scurry out of reach. So, owls have soft-edged feathers that help them fly quietly and large wings that allow them to glide with few wingbeats.

White spruce cones

Red maple seeds

As fall approaches, most of the forest's trees have developed seeds. Pines and many other evergreens hide their seeds within egg-shaped cones. When the cones ripen, the seeds blow with the wind. Broad-leaved trees bear their seeds inside fruits. Sometimes the fruits are sweet, like apples or cherries, but often they are hard and woody. Acorns and beechnuts, loved by squirrels and chipmunks, are actually the fruits of oak and beech trees. Red maples have double-winged fruits called samaras. They will whirl to the ground like helicopter wings.

The large leathery ball on the ground is a kind of mushroom called a puffball, and it is named well! Press gently on a ripe one, and spores will puff out like a cloud of smoke. Spores are like microscopic seeds produced in great numbers by mushrooms, ferns, and some other plants. They are so light that the wind can take them many miles—sometimes all the way around the world! Inside a puffball are millions, even billions, of spores. But very few will survive, fortunately.

Puffball

The coming of crisp, cool weather turns the forest into a riot of color. Some of the dazzling reds and yellows that appear in autumn have been in the leaves all along. But in spring and summer they are masked by the leaf's green color.

The green color is caused by something called chlorophyll. Chlorophyll helps plants turn sunlight into food. When the days and nights turn cool, the leaf stops making chlorophyll and the brilliant colors of fall show through.

At this time of year, many animals are busy preparing for winter. Many fatten themselves while fruit and nuts abound, and some store food for the months ahead.

Maple leaves

Chipmunk

Salamanders

Once winter sets in, bears and chipmunks hibernate, but they are not the only creatures who survive the winter by becoming inactive.

Salamanders and American toads burrow beneath the leaves into the rich, soft soil of the forest floor, where they sluggishly wait out the winter. Next spring, warming temperatures will stir them from their sleep.

American toad

Ice on a branch

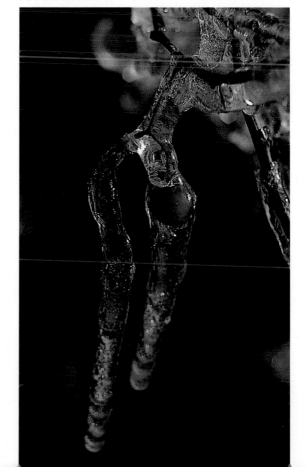

Winter's frigid days threaten many forest inhabitants. To some, a heavy blanket of snow is a blessing. It insulates hibernators from icy winds, and can even protect many active animals who burrow into the snowbanks.

Gray squirrel

For a squirrel, even shriveled fruit is a rare treat during the hardest time of year. But for those of us who can return to warm homes with plenty of food, a visit to the winter woods with its cloak of snow or shimmering coat of ice is an experience of great beauty.